What We Have in Common

A Brim Coloring Book

Written by Jane Landey
Edited by David Austin
Drawings by David Austin and Jane Austin
Copyright©2017
All rights reserved.

Printed in U.S.A.

Introduction

What We Have in Common. Brim Coloring Books enable children to color the drawings as they read along! The books display the similarities of related animals. In this series, Turtle and Tortoise are compared. The facts enable children to appreciate common values. Thus, imbibing in them an interest towards animals which could help them appreciate what they have in common with one another.

THE TURTLE

AND

THE TORTOISE

The turtle and the tortoise
have things in common.
They have big shells that protect
their bodies. The turtle lives in
water while the tortoise lives on
land.

A turtle and a tortoise meet on a bright day and when the sky is clear.

I am a turtle.

I am a tortoise.

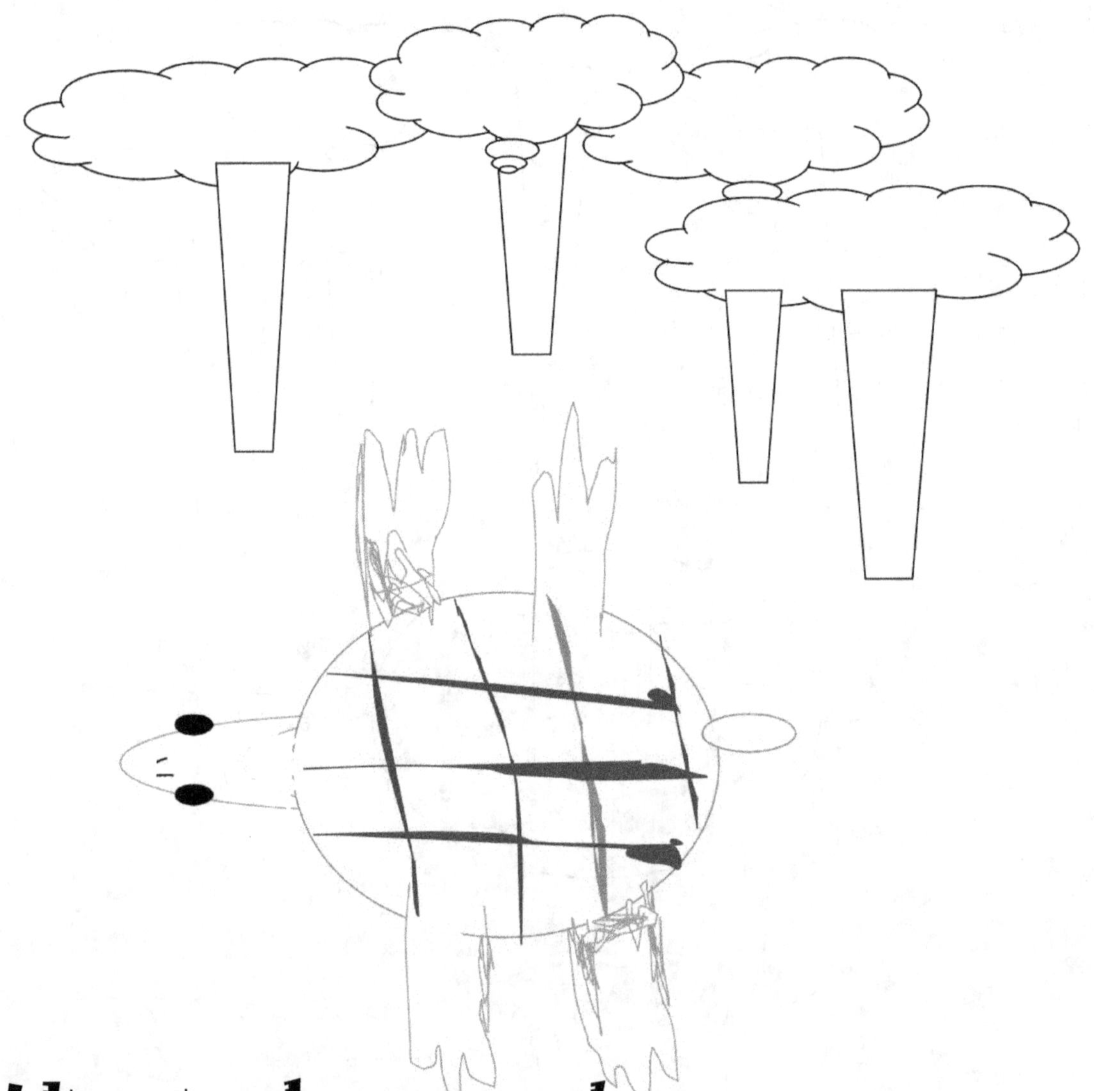

I live in the water but
sometimes I come on land.

I live on the land.

I have a cracked shell.

I have a cracked shell too.

I have sharp nails.

So do I.

I have a small head.

I have a small head too!

I can hide my head.

I can too!

Look at me do it.

Look at me do it too!

I have a short tail.

My tail is short too!

I can hide under weeds in
the water.

I can hide under rocks, wood
or stone too!

I am a jester!

I am a trickster!

A turtle loves to swim.

A tortoise loves to run.

Mister Turtle has other friends.

Mister Tortoise has other friends too.

A jelly fish and crab like turtle.

A hare and rabbit like tortoise too!

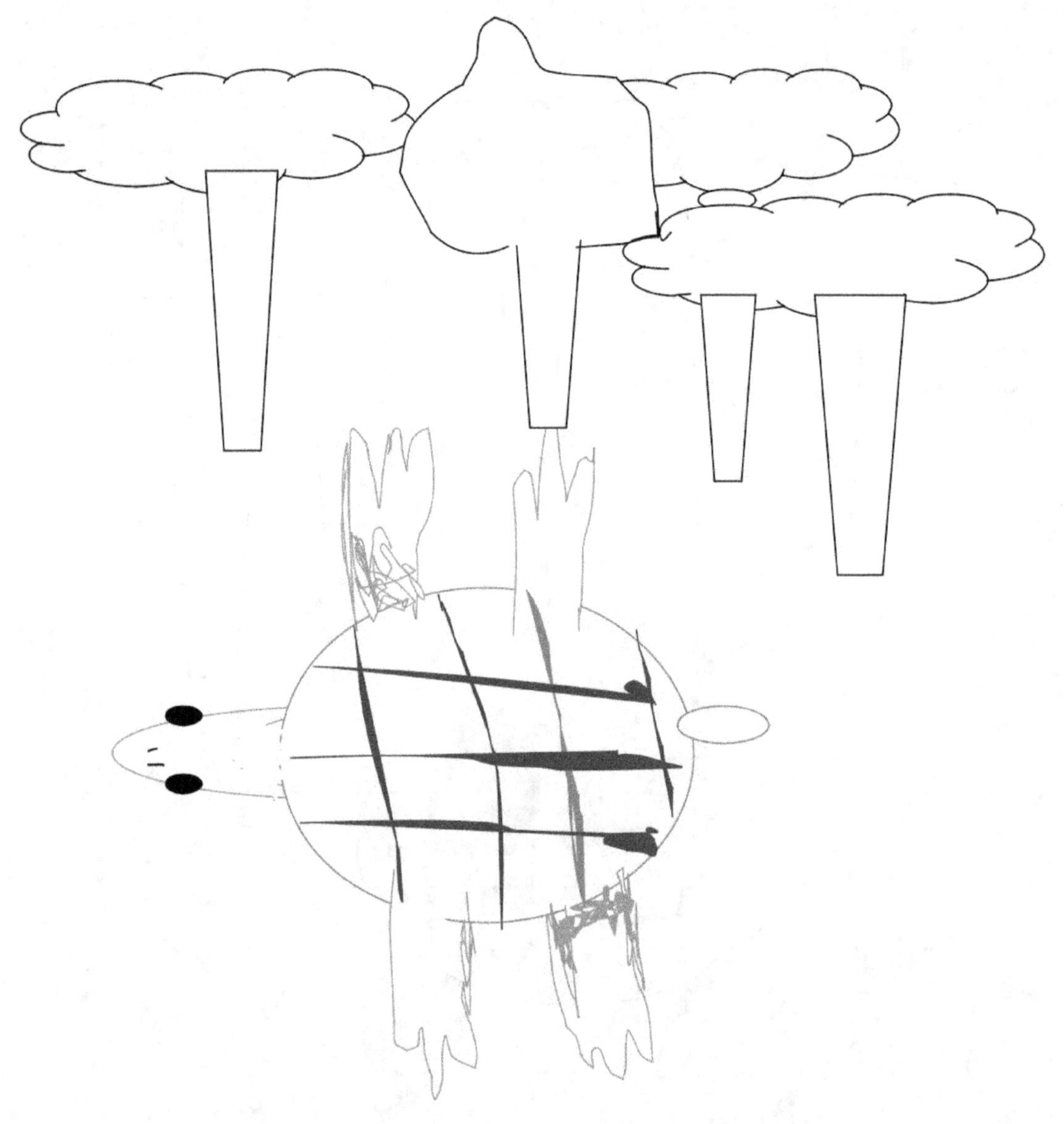

A turtle cannot run fast.

A tortoise cannot run fast either!

A turtle cannot climb a wall.

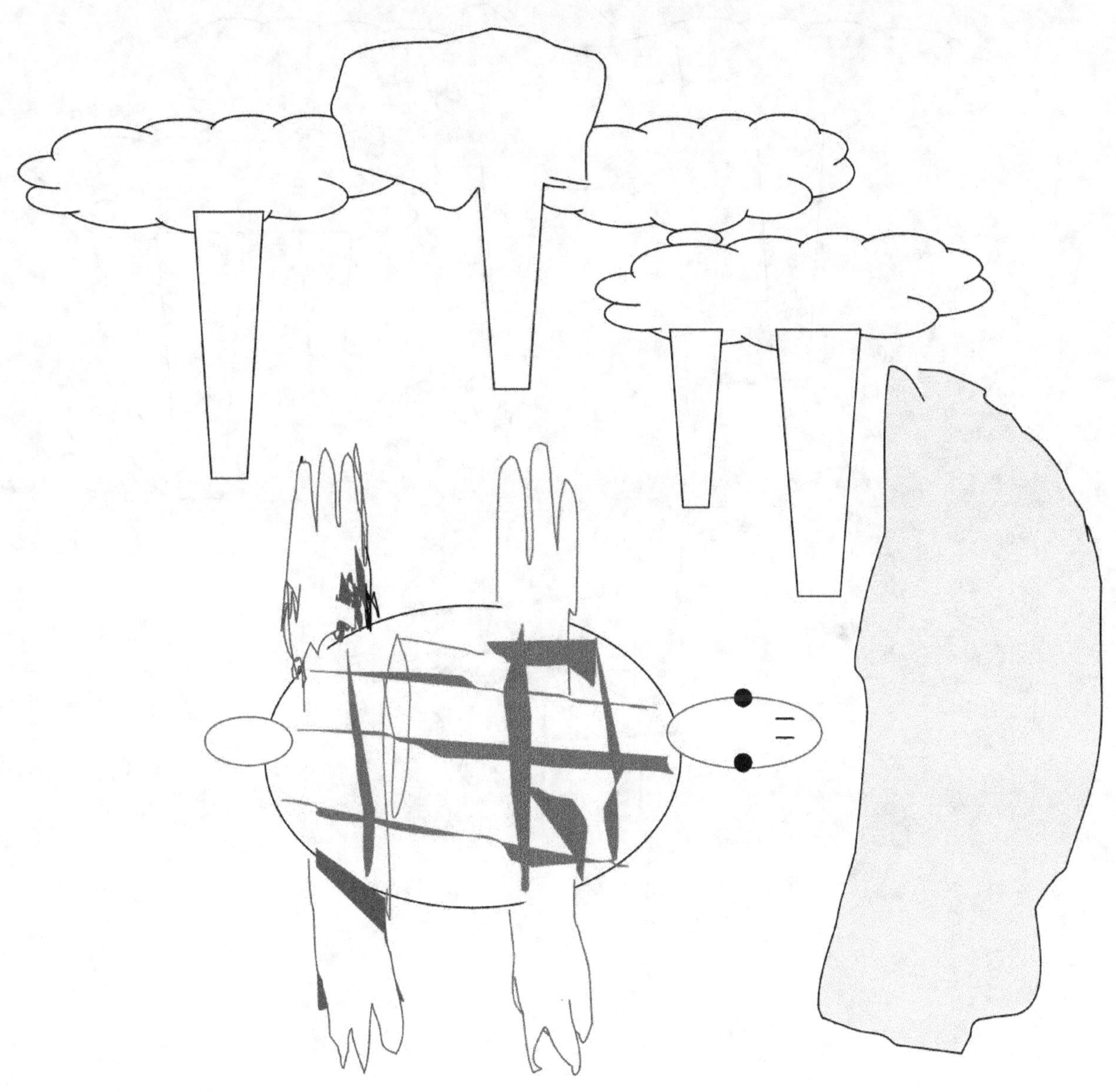

A tortoise cannot climb a wall either!

A turtle can play in the soil.

A tortoise can play in the soil too!

What We Have in Common Brim Coloring Books

Crocodile and Alligator
Turtle and Tortoise
Starfish and Octopus
Worm and Snake
Turkey and Vulture
Ostrich and Emu
Weka and Kiwi
Bat and Rat
Camel and Llama
Duck and Pelican
Kangaroo and Wallaby
Pig and Tapir
Skunk and Squirrel
Hedge and Anteater
Cat and Owl
Elephant and Rhinoceros
Dog and fox
Buffalo and Bull
Leopard and Cheetah
Horse and Zebra

www.ingramcontent.com/pod-product-compliance
Lightning Source LLC
Chambersburg PA
CBHW081255250726
48654CB00012B/1619